For Jack ♡

Sally
The
Grocery Store Cat

with love and gratitude,
MaryAnne Polich

Written and Illustrated by MaryAnne M. Polich
Boston, Massachusetts, USA

Proceeds from the sale of this book will be donated to
The Rescue House (rescuehouse.org) in Encinitas, CA,
a non-profit, volunteer-based, cat rescue organization;
as well as local animal rescue organizations
with similar non-profit status.

Fourth printing March 2019
Third printing November 2018
Second printing July 2018
First printing May 2018

Published by MaryAnne M. Polich
www.singingcatlover.com

With eternal love and gratitude for Sally, and for all our beloved cats
who are with her in Heaven—Mittens, Molly, Betsy, Amy, Oliver, Philip, Clara, Mikey,
Judy, Hazel and Edith—who have brought so much love into our lives. They will always
be in our hearts. And for the precious cats that we are blessed with now—
Madeleine, William, Gladys, Francis and Tommy,
and the future "fur-babies" we will have.

I am forever grateful for my husband, Bob, for his unending support
and love for me and for all our cats.

With thanks to Mary H. for always being here for me and offering her
talented perspective, advice and help with design.

With thanks to Carrie B. for supporting and encouraging me
to complete my dream of finishing this project.

This book is dedicated to the memory of our dear friend and veterinarian
Dr. Paul Nelson Fenner. We were blessed to have his friendship, and his love
and care for our kitties. We miss him very much, and we know he is with
all the animals in Heaven that he cared for on earth.

...until we all meet again.

Sally was a grocery store cat.

At least, that's where she was found the day she was rescued,
and later adopted by her forever family.

It was a warm sunny day in August and a little black cat,
with orange colored patches and a few spots of white,
wandered into a neighborhood grocery store.
She didn't know how she got there, but she knew she was lost.

She was very frightened by all the big, noisy grocery carts
and people racing up and down the aisles,
and she didn't know where to go!

Thank goodness a nice lady saw her and picked her up!

The lady asked the little cat where she was from
and if her owner was nearby.
The kitty just purred and cuddled in the lady's arms.

The lady asked the people in the store if they had seen this kitty before, but nobody had.

She wasn't sure what to do, but she knew
she had to help this scared little kitty find her way home.

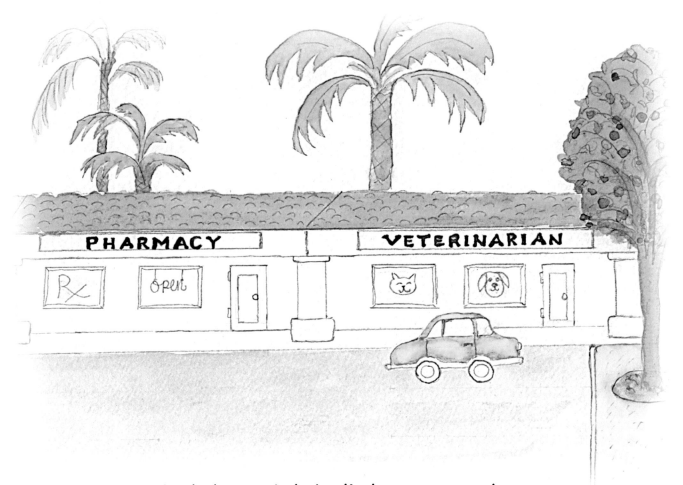

So, the lady carried the little cat out to her car.
Then she noticed a sign across the parking lot that said
VETERINARIAN and she thought, "hmmm, maybe they can help"
and she drove over with the kitty.

A veterinarian is a doctor for animals.
Every pet should have a veterinarian just like people have doctors.

The veterinarian and his wife were both working.
They were very kind and said they would
try to help find the kitty's owner.

Then the lady took the little cat home and kept her over the weekend,
hoping someone would see the signs she had put up.
But no one was looking for the kitty.
Not even one person called.
The lady was sad that no one was missing her.

The little cat knew she was very lucky to have been found that day.
She could have been hit by a car, or hurt by another animal
or a mean person if she was left on her own.

Well, it didn't take long before the nice lady and her husband had fallen in love with the little cat. They really wanted to adopt her. But they waited a little longer to see if the kitty's owner would see the signs and call.

A few weeks went by and the little cat realized
that she had found her true home
with her new sisters, Molly and Betsy.

The lady and her husband adopted the little cat and
they decided to name her Sally.

Now that they adopted Sally, they knew they needed to take her to a doctor for a check-up and vaccinations. So they went back to Dr. Fenner, the nice veterinarian they had met.

Dr. Fenner examined Sally. He looked in her mouth, in her ears and
eyes and checked her body to make sure everything felt normal.
He thought she was about six months old and had not been spayed.
This is an operation to keep her from having kittens.

The veterinarian said,
"If Sally had kittens it would be hard
to find good homes for them." He explained,
"there are so many homeless cats, dogs and other
animals in shelters and on the streets all over the world.
It's impossible to find a home for all of them."

"That's why all pets should be spayed or neutered."

He suggested that when a family decides to adopt a pet,
they can go to an animal shelter or rescue group to find their new
furry family member. Hopefully one day all the homeless animals
will have their true home and forever family.

Molly and Betsy were happy to have a new sister. They all loved to play and snuggle together. Sally never wanted to go outside again. She was happy to be an indoor cat like Betsy and Molly. They showed Sally all the fun hiding places and toys to play with, and cozy spots to take cat-naps.

Sally was so happy that
the nice lady found her
at the grocery store.
Her big adventure had
the kind of happy ending
every lost pet wishes for.

Little Sally had indeed found her true home
and her loving forever family.

The End

Meet the real Sally, Molly and Betsy.

Sally

Molly and Betsy

These are our kitties that we've rescued over the years.

Mittens

Molly

Betsy

Sally

Amy

Oliver

Philip

Judy

Each of them has been a blessing in our lives.

Madeleine

William

Edith

Mikey

Clara

Hazel

Gladys

Francis

Tommy

41663683R00015

Made in the USA
Middletown, DE
09 April 2019